THE MOON SEEMS TO CHANGE

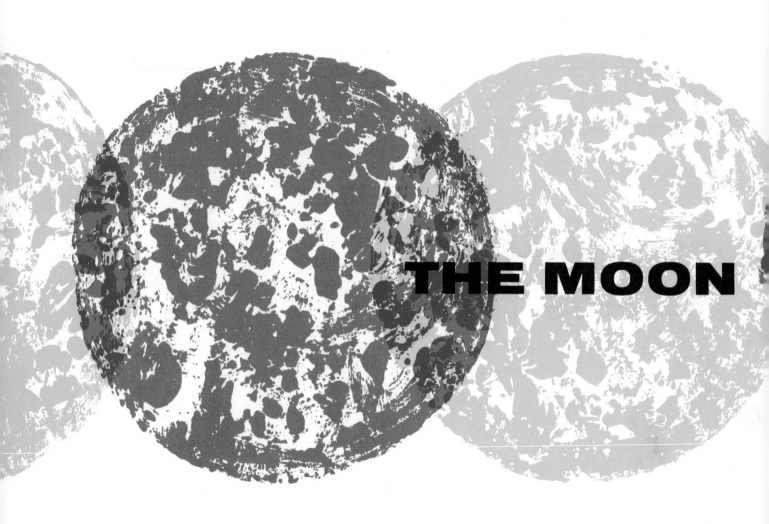

THE MOON

SEEMS TO CHANGE

by **Franklyn M. Branley** and illustrated by **Helen Borten**

THOMAS Y. CROWELL COMPANY · NEW YORK

 ® LIBRARY EDITION

LET'S-READ-AND-FIND-OUT SCIENCE BOOKS

Editors: *DR. ROMA GANS,* Professor Emeritus of Childhood Education, Teachers College, Columbia University

DR. FRANKLYN M. BRANLEY, Chairman of The American Museum—Hayden Planetarium, consultant on science in elementary education

*AVAILABLE IN SPANISH

REC Library Edition reprinted with the permission of Thomas Y. Crowell Company

Responsive Environments Corp., Englewood Cliffs, N. J. 07632

THE MOON SEEMS TO CHANGE

U.S. 1815685

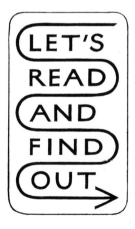

This is the moon.

The moon is big.

A house is big. The moon is much bigger.

A mountain is big. The moon is much bigger.

The moon is BIG.

The moon is far away.

You cannot drive to the moon. There is no road.

But if you could drive to the moon it would take almost a year.

You would have to drive a car all day for ten months.

The moon is very far away.

10 *Months*

The moon looks smooth.

The moon is not smooth.

There are high places and low places on the moon.

The low places are big holes. They are called craters.

The high places are the walls around the craters.

There are many craters on the moon.

The moon
has no water or air.
It has no rain.

It has no trees or grass.

The moon has no flowers.

The moon has no cats or dogs.

The moon has no birds.

The moon has no fish or frogs.

The moon has no boys or girls.

The moon has no big people.
The moon has no plants
or animals of any kind.

9

The moon turns.

You can see how. Stand on one spot and turn around.

The moon turns the same way.

The moon takes a month to turn all the way around.

You can turn around much faster!

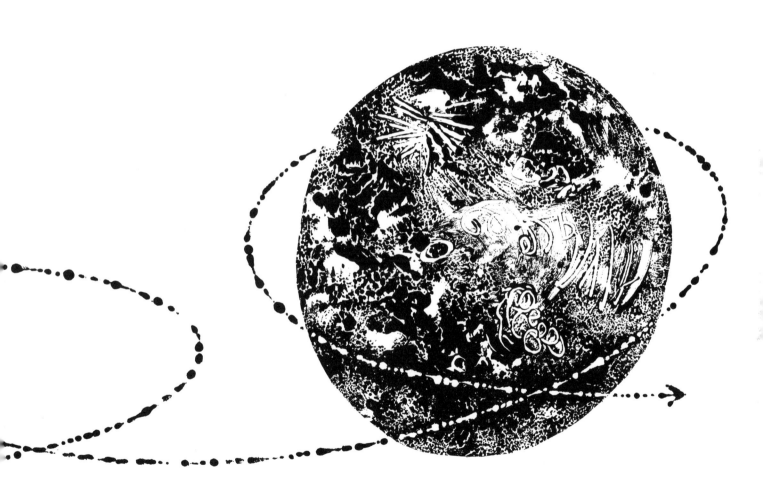

The sun shines on half of the moon at one time.
That half has day.
That half of the moon is very hot.
It is too hot to live on.

13

At the same time the other half of the moon is dark.
That half has night.
That half of the moon is very cold.
It is too cold to live on.

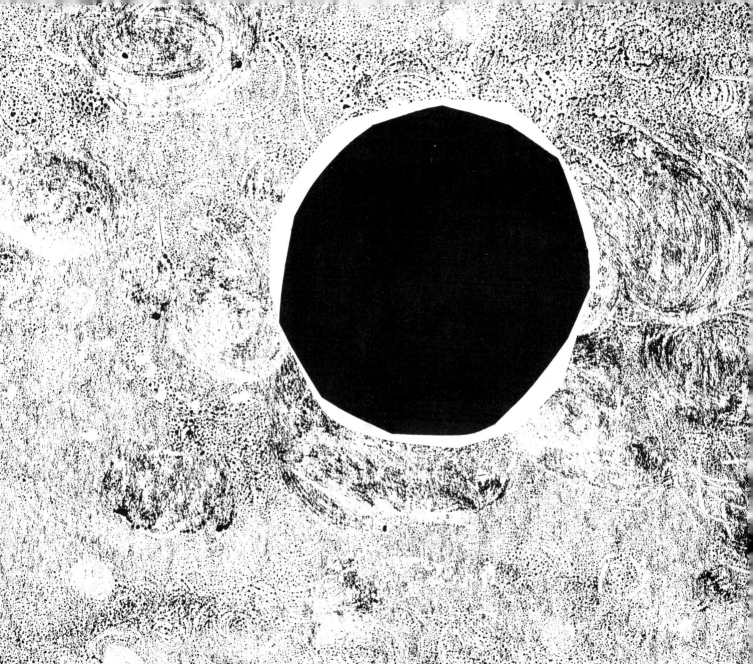

Look at the moon tonight.
It may look like this;

or like this,

or like this.

Maybe
you will not see the moon at all.

The moon seems to change.
The moon really does not change.

This is why the moon seems to change.

The moon goes around the earth. Sometimes we see all of the day side of the moon.

Sometimes we see part of the day side of the moon.

When the day side is turned away from the earth, people on the earth cannot see the moon.

Do this experiment. It will show you why the moon
seems to change.

Stand with your back to a lamp. Pretend the lamp is
the sun.

Pretend your head is the earth.

Hold a ball in front of you. Hold it higher than your
head. The ball is the moon.

Now you see the part lighted by the lamp. You see
the day side of the moon.

Turn so your side is toward the lamp. Hold the ball
in front of you.
Now you see only part of the lighted side of the ball.
You see only part of the day side of the moon.
Turn toward the lamp. Hold the ball in front of you.
Now you see none of the lighted side of the ball. You
see none of the moon.

Watch the moon in the sky. Watch it every night for two weeks.

The moon seems to change from night to night.

When the moon looks round, you see all the lighted half. (See picture number 1.)

When you see the moon as it is in picture number 2, you see part of the lighted half.

Sometimes you cannot see the moon at all. The lighted half is turned away from you.

1

2

Now you know:

        The moon is big.

        There is no air or water on the moon.

There are no plants or animals on the moon.
The moon is hot during its daytime.

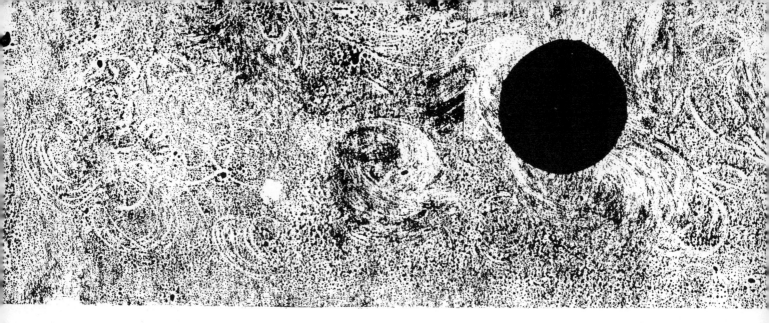

The moon is cold during its night.

The moon goes around the earth.

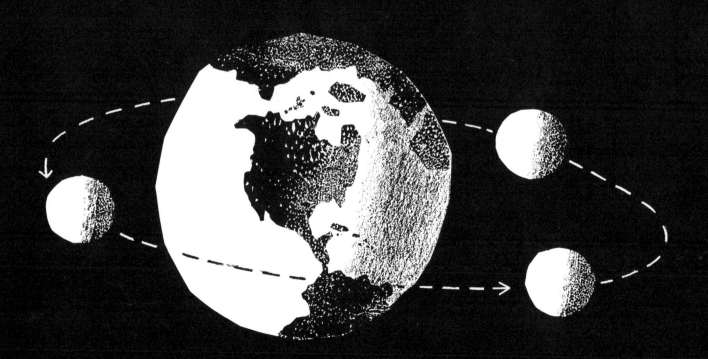

Watch the moon from night to night.
See how the moon seems to change.
Now you know that it really doesn't.

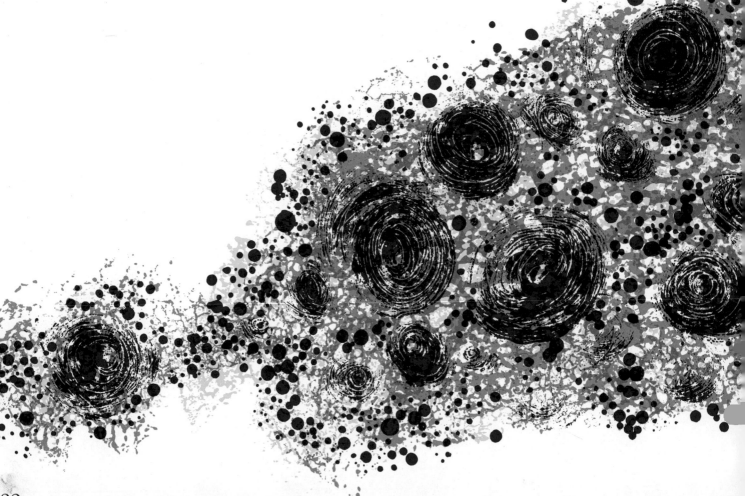

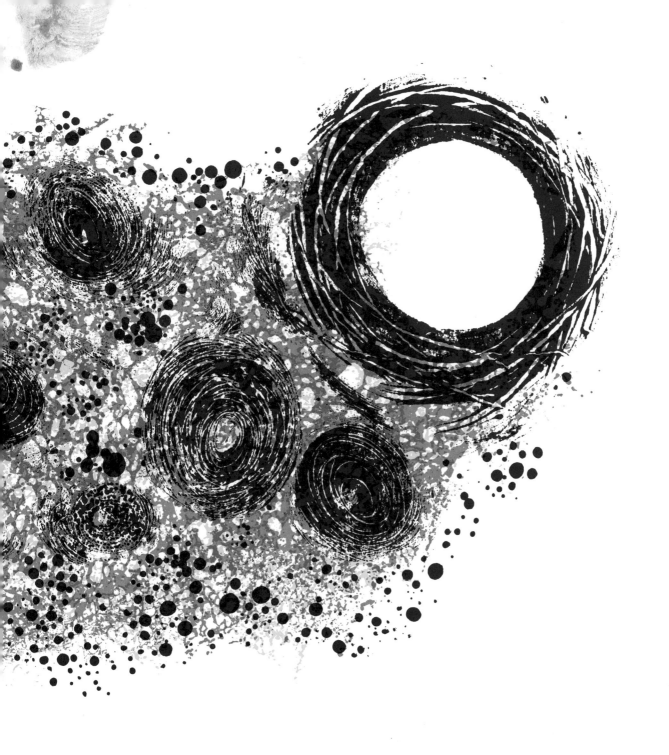

ABOUT THE AUTHOR

FRANKLYN M. BRANLEY is Astronomer and Chairman at the American Museum-Hayden Planetarium in New York City. For many years he has helped children learn scientific facts and principles at an early age without impairing their sense of wonder about the world they live in. Before coming to the Planetarium, Dr. Branley taught science at many grade levels including the lower elementary grades, high school, college, and graduate school.

Dr. Branley received his training for teaching at the State Teachers College in New Paltz, New York, at New York University, and Columbia University. He lives with his family in Woodcliff Lake, New Jersey.

ABOUT THE ARTIST

HELEN BORTEN has illustrated several books for children and is the author and illustrator of two others: *Do You See What I See?* and *Do You Hear What I Hear?*

Mrs. Borten was born in Philadelphia, Pennsylvania, and was graduated from the Philadelphia Museum College of Art. She lives with her husband and two sons, Peter and Laurence, in Lafayette Hill, Pennsylvania.